Axioms of Kwame Nkrumah

The secret of life is to have no fear

By the same author

Africa Must Unite

Challenge of the Congo

Class Struggle in Africa

Consciencism

Dark Days in Ghana

*Ghana: The Autobiography of
   Kwame Nkrumah*

Handbook of Revolutionary Warfare

I Speak of Freedom

Neo-colonialism

Revolutionary Path

Rhodesia File

*The Struggle Continues —
   6 Panaf pamphlets*

Towards Colonial Freedom

Voice from Conakry

All available from Panaf Books

Axioms of Kwame Nkrumah

International Edition

Panaf Books

Panaf Books

75 Weston Street
London SE1 3RS

First published 1967.
Reprinted 1969, 1972, 2002, 2003.

ISBN   0 901787 00 0

Printed in the UK
by Antony Rowe Ltd, Eastbourne

Contents

Africa 1
African Personality 3
African Revolution 5
African Unity 7
African Resources 20
Aid 20
Apartheid 21
Army 22
Balkanisation 23
Black Power 24
Capitalism 26
Civil Service 28
Co-existence 30
Colonialism 31
Commonwealth 36
Consciencism 37
Convention People's Party 38
Development Plans 46
Economic Independence 51
Economic Unity 52
Education 53
Freedom 55
Ghana 62

Imperialism	64
Independence	69
Industrialisation	77
Nationalism	80
Neo-colonialism	82
Nuclear Weapons	92
One Man — One Vote	93
One Party State	95
Peace	98
People's Militia	99
The People	100
Philosophy	103
Positive Action	104
Propaganda	106
Racialism	106
Religion	107
Revolution	108
Revolutionary War	110
Socialism	113
"Third World"	119
Trade Unionism	120
Unitary Government	121
United Nations Organisation	122
Women	123

Africa

AFRICA is marching forward to freedom and no power on earth can halt her now.
> Speech in National Assembly, Accra. 16 December 1959

What are the aspirations of Africans? Above all, they desire to regain their independence. They desire independence and to live in peace. They desire to use their freedom to raise the standard of living of their peoples. They desire to use their freedom to create a union of African states on the continent, and thus neutralise the evil effects of the artificial boundaries imposed by the imperial powers and promote unity of action in all fields. These are Africa's ideals.
> Speech at symposium held by the English Speaking Union in Central Hall, Westminster, London May 1960

It has often been said that Africa is poor. What nonsense! It is not Africa that is poor. It is the Africans, who are impoverished by centuries of exploitation and domination.
> Speech in National Assembly, Accra. 8 August 1960

Only Africa can fight for its destiny. In this struggle we shall not reject the assistance and support of our friends, but we will yield to no enemy, however strong.

> The same

Africa wants her freedom, Africa must be free. It is a simple call, but it is also a signal lighting a red warning to those who would tend to ignore it.

> Speech in UN General Assembly, New York. 23 September 1960

Africa needs a new type of citizen, a dedicated, modest, honest, informed man. A man who submerges self in service to the nation and mankind. A man who abhors greed and detests vanity. A new type of man whose humility is his strength and whose integrity is his greatness.

> *Africa Must Unite*, 1963, p. 130

Africa is a paradox which illustrates and highlights neo-colonialism. Her earth is rich, yet the products that come from above and below the soil continue to enrich, not Africans pre–dominantly, but groups and individuals who operate to Africa's impoverishment.

> *Neo-colonialism*, p. 1

The continent of Africa is compact, self-sufficient and unique. Geopolitically it forms a single unit with its own personality.

Dark Days in Ghana, 1968

African Personality

We feel that there is much the world can learn from those of us who belong to what we might term the pre-technological societies. There are values which we must not sacrifice unheedingly in pursuit of material progress. That is why we say that self-government is not an end in itself. We have to work hard to evolve new patterns, new social customs, new attitudes to life, so that while we seek the material, cultural and economic advancement of our people, while we raise their standard of life, we shall not sacrifice their fundamental happiness.

Motion of Destiny speech in National Assembly, Accra. 10 July 1953

The desire of the African people themselves to unite and to assert their personality in the context of the African community has made itself felt everywhere.

Speech of welcome to representatives of African Trade Unions meeting in Accra to organise an All-African Trade Union Federation, 5 November 1959

Ghana's independence is meaningless unless it is linked up with the total liberation of Africa and with the projection of the African personality in the international community.

> Speech made in Accra. March 1960

When I speak of the African genius, I mean something different from negritude, something not apologetical, but dynamic. Negritude consists in a mere literary affectation and style which piles up word upon word and image upon image with occasional reference to Africa and things African. I do not mean a vague brotherhood based on a criterion of colour, or on the idea that Africans have no reasoning but only a sensitivity. By the African genius I mean something positive, our socialist conception of society, the efficiency and validity of our traditional statecraft, our highly developed code of morals, our hospitality and our purposeful energy.

> Speech at the opening of the Institute of African Studies, Accra. 25 October 1963

It is only in conditions of total freedom and independence from foreign rule and interference that the aspirations of our people will see real fulfilment and the African genius find its best expression.

> The same

The African personality is ... defined by the cluster of humanist principles which underlie the traditional African society.

Consciencism, p. 79

We are doing everything to revive our culture; but if this revival is to endure it must be based on strong moral and spiritual foundations. Our moral and spiritual qualities should not lag behind the progress we are making in the economic field.

Address to the National Assembly, Accra. 12 June 1965

African Revolution

When we turn to the study of modern Africa we are again confronted with the necessity of thinking in continental terms. The liberation movements which have emerged in Africa have clearly all been aspects of a single African revolution. They have to be understood from the standpoint of the special kinds of colonial situation within which they have had to operate and the special problems which they have had to face.

Speech at the opening of the Institute of African Studies. 25 October 1963

Crises will occur as the African revolutionary struggle continues to gain momentum. We must be prepared to deal with them. Now is the time to make a concerted and sustained effort to achieve an All-African Union Government, without which final victory of the African Revolution will be incomplete.

Challenge of the Congo, Preface, p. xi

Because attempts to achieve political and economic independence and to advance on the road towards continental unity have been consistently and insidiously sabotaged by neo-colonialist manoeuvres, it is no longer possible, indeed it would be suicidal to combat such dangerous and ruthless forces by the old methods of peaceful persuasion and compromise. For years, a virtual state of war has existed in Africa between the developing independent states, and the foreign interests determined to maintain and even strengthen their stranglehold on the economic life of our continent. This "war" must now come into the open and be fought and won in the military sense if Africa is ever to achieve her full development.

The same, p. x

As a continental nation we are young, strong and resilient. The cohesive planning of our struggle and the combined strength of our will to win will do the rest. Africa is one: and this battle must be fought and won continentally.

Handbook of Revolutionary Warfare, Preface

African Unity

Today we are one. If in the past the Sahara divided us, now it unites us and an injury to one is an injury to all.

Speech at Conference of Independent African States, Accra. 15 April 1958

To many people, the unity of African states which we regard as the primary basis of our African policy appears visionary and unattainable. We do not hold this view. The unity of African states can be a reality and it will be achieved earlier than many of us suppose.

Speech in Dublin. 18 May 1960

If we do not formulate plans for unity and take active steps to form political union, we will soon be fighting and warring among ourselves with imperialists and colonialists standing behind the screen and pulling vicious wires, to make us cut each other's throats for the sake of their diabolical purposes in Africa.

> Speech at the closing session of the Casablanca Conference. 7 January 1961

I can see no security for African states unless African leaders like ourselves have realised beyond all doubt that salvation for Africa lies in unity.

> The same

Divided we are weak: united, Africa could become one of the greatest forces for good in the world.

> *I Speak of Freedom*, Preface, p. xii

To suggest that the time is not yet ripe for considering a political union of Africa is to evade the facts and ignore realities in Africa today.

> The same, p. xiii

Critics often refer to the wide differences in culture, language and ideas in various parts of Africa. This is true, but the essential fact remains that we are all Africans, and have a common interest in the independence of Africa ... . If the need for political union is agreed by us all, then the will to create it is born; and where there's a will there's a way.

The same

We have to prove that greatness is not to be measured in stock-piles of atom bombs. I believe strongly and sincerely that with the deep-rooted wisdom and dignity, the innate respect for human lives, the intense humanity that is our heritage, the African race, united under one federal government, will emerge not as just another world bloc to flaunt its wealth and strength, but as a Great Power whose greatness is indestructible because it is built not on fear, envy and suspicion, nor won at the expense of others, but founded on hope, trust, friendship and directed to the good of all mankind.

The same, p. xiv

No nation can afford to live in isolation and hope to preserve its sovereignty and independence in the present circumstances of the world.

Undated Speech

I, my Party and Government are completely devoted to the achievement of the political and economic unification of Africa. This is not an idle dream. It is not impossible.

I see it; I feel it; it is real; indeed I am living in it already.

New Year Message, 1963

If we are to remain free, if we are to enjoy the full benefits of Africa's rich resources, we must unite to plan for our total defence and the full exploitation of our material and human means, in the full interest of all our people. "To go it alone" will limit our horizons, curtail our expectations and threaten our liberty.

Africa Must Unite, Introduction, p. xvii

Our freedom stands open to danger just as long as the independent states of Africa remain apart.

The same

I am convinced that the forces making for unity far outweigh those which divide us. In meeting fellow Africans from all parts of the continent I am constantly impressed by how much we have in common. It is not just our colonial past, or the fact that we have aims in common, it is something which goes far deeper. I can best describe it as a sense of oneness in that we are Africans.

The same, p. 132

African Unity

In a world divided into hostile camps and warring factions, Africa cannot stand divided without going to the wall.

> The same, p. 147

I have often been accused of pursuing "a policy of the impossible". But I cannot believe in the impossibility of achieving African union any more than I could ever have thought of the impossibility of attaining African freedom.

> The same, p. 170

Pan-Africa and not Eurafrica should be our watchword, and the guide to our policies.

> The same, p. 187

The forces that unite us are intrinsic and greater than the superimposed influences that keep us apart. These are the forces that we must enlist and cement for the sake of the trusting millions who look to us, their leaders, to take them out of the poverty, ignorance and disorder left by colonialism into an ordered unity in which freedom and amity can flourish amidst plenty.

> The same, p. 221

There is no time to waste. The longer we wait the stronger will be the hold on Africa of neo-colonialism and imperialism. A Union Government for Africa does not mean the loss of sovereignty by independent African states. A Union Government will rather strengthen the sovereignty of the individual states within the Union.

> Speech made in Accra, 24 May 1964

We cannot save ourselves except through the unity of our continent based on common action through a Continental Union Government. Only a united Africa under a Union Government can cure us of our economic ills and lift us out of our despair and frustration.

> Speech at the Cairo Summit Conference, 26 July 1964

We look forward to the early establishment of a Continental Union Government of Africa which will throw the whole weight and might of a united Africa to the support of world peace and prosperity.

> Address to the National Assembly, 26 March 1965

There is a battle to be fought, there are obstacles to be overcome. There is a world struggle for human dignity to be won. Let us address ourselves seriously to the supreme tasks that lie ahead. To accomplish these aims, Africa must unite.

> The same

All our efforts and aspirations at home must be geared to one purpose and one grand objective. We believe that by one mighty continental effort the African states can generate a united force that can brave any imperialist storm, and break its way through the obstacles of neo-colonialist obstruction. In this task all of us, parliamentarians, politicians, academicians, journalists, workers, farmers — all sections of our population — have a part to play.

> The same

If Africa was united, no major power bloc would attempt to subdue it by limited war because, from the very nature of limited war, what can be achieved by it is itself limited. It is only where small states exist that it is possible, by landing a few thousand marines or by financing a mercenary force, to secure a decisive result.

> *Neo-colonialism*, Introduction, p. xi

A continent like Africa, however much it increases its agricultural output, will not benefit unless it is sufficiently politically and economically united to force the developed world to pay it a fair price for its cash crops.

The same, p. 9

In the same way as mass pressure made it impossible for an African leader to oppose independence, so today mass pressure makes it impossible for him openly to oppose African unity.

The same, p. 24

The case for African unity is very strong and the instinct of the mass of the people right.

The same

Economic unity to be effective must be accompanied by political unity. The two are inseparable, each necessary for the future greatness of our continent, and the full development of our resources.

The same, p. 30

Unity is the first requisite for destroying neo-colonialism. Primary and basic is the need for a Union Government on the much divided continent of Africa.

The same, p. 253

African Unity

No one would suggest that if all the peoples of Africa combined to establish their unity their decision could be revoked by the forces of neo-colonialism. On the contrary, faced with a new situation, those who practise neo-colonialism would adjust themselves to this new balance of world forces in exactly the same way as the capitalist world in the past adjusted itself to any change in the balance of power.

The same, p. 259

Only a united Africa can redeem its past glory and renew and reinforce its strength for the realisation of its destiny. We are today the richest and yet the poorest of continents, but in unity our continent could smile in a new era of prosperity and power.

Undated Speech

Africa must unite. We have before us not only an opportunity but a historic duty. It is in our hands to join our strength, taking sustenance from our diversity, honouring our rich and varied traditions and culture but acting together for the protection and benefit of us all.

Speech in the National Assembly, 22 March 1965

I do not believe that the economic development of Africa can reach an effective stage until Africa's human and material resources have been mobilised under a Continental Union Government of Africa. But I do believe (and nothing that has happened or can happen, will swerve me from my belief), that the emergence of a Continental Government of Africa will immediately make the independent states of Africa a mighty world influence. We shall then be in a far better position to liberate our brothers in colonial bondage and rule, to drive out imperialism and neo-colonialism from our continent, to make us a powerful ally of the Asian peoples in their own struggles against imperialism, and to make us an effective force for world peace.

Speech at the Fourth Afro-Asian Solidarity Conference at Winneba, 10 May 1961[5]

An area which is united must have far greater power than the sum of the component units of which it was originally comprised. If the United States of America had remained divided into separate states, would these states collectively have had the authority in the councils of the world of the United States Government today? If the component republics of revolutionary Russia had not come together to make up the Union of Soviet Socialist Republics, would Russia be the force in the world that it is today? A United Africa could be as great a force in world affairs as either the United States of America, or the Soviet Union.

> Address to the National Assembly, 3 September 1965

I am prepared to serve in a political union of free African states under any African leader who is able to offer the proper guidance in this great issue of our time.

> Undated Speech

Africa is ripe for a new revolution — an armed revolution. A new phase of the African Revolution has been reached. This revolution must overcome and triumph over imperialism, racialism and neo-colonialism. It must finally usher in the total emancipation and the political unification of our continent. Africa must be free; Africa must be united.

> Broadcast from Conakry to the people of Ghana, 10 April 1966

There are likely to be more coups and rebellions in Africa as long as imperialists and neo-colonialists are able to exploit our weaknesses. Unless we unite and deal with neo-colonialism on a Pan-African basis, they will continue to try to undermine our independence, and draw us again into spheres of influence comparable to the original carve up of Africa arranged at the Berlin Conference of 1884.

Challenge of the Congo, Preface, p. x

The concept of African unity embraces the fundamental needs and characteristics of African civilisation and ideology, and at the same time satisfies all the conditions necessary for an accelerated economic and technological advance. Such maximum development would ensure a rational utilisation of the material resources and human potential of our continent along the lines of an integrated economy, and within complementary sectors of production, eliminating all unnecessary forms of competition, economic alienation and duplication.

Handbook of Revolutionary Warfare, p. 26

African unity gives an indispensable continental dimension to the concept of the African nation.

The same, p. 27

At the core of the concept of African unity lies socialism and the socialist definition of the new African society.

> The same, p. 28

Without political unity, African states will never commit themselves to full economic integration, which is the only productive form of integration able to develop our great resources fully for the well-being of the African people as a whole.

> The same, p. 40

The lack of political unity places inter-African economic institutions at the mercy of powerful, foreign commercial interests, and sooner or later these will use such institutions as funnels through which to pour money for the continued exploitation of Africa.

> The same

The resistance of the masses of Africa to imperialist aggression grows daily. African freedom and unity have become their watchwords. In that alone lies their fulfilment.

> *Dark Days in Ghana*, p. 158

African Resources

If Africa's multiple resources were used in her own development, they could place her among the modernised continents of the world. But her resources have been, and still are being used for the greater development of overseas interests.

Neo-Colonialism, p. 2

Africa is still paramountly an uncharted continent economically, and the withdrawal of the colonial rulers from political control is interpreted as a signal for the descent of the international monopolies upon the continent's natural resources.

The same, p. 109

Aid

Conscious of our responsibilities towards Africa and its people, we must guard against any attempts by the imperialists, colonialists and neo-colonialists to use financial aid as a means of economic infiltration and ultimately of political subjection.

Note to Heads of all Independent African States. June 1962

"Aid" ... to a neo-colonial State is merely a revolving credit, paid by the neo-colonial master, passing through the neo-colonial State and returning to the neo-colonial master in the form of increased profits.

Neo-Colonialism, Introduction, p. xv

Before the decline of colonialism what today is known as aid was simply foreign investment.

The same, p. 51

Apartheid

Theinterest of humanity compels every nation to take steps against such inhumanity and barbarity and to act in concert to eliminate it from the world.

Speech to the General Assembly of the UN, New York. 23 September 1960

The untenable claim of a minority in South Africa is steadily building a wall of intense hate which will result in the most violent and regrettable consequences in the future unless this minority abandons the iniquitous racial policy which it pursues.

The same

Wherever there is the possibility of conflict arising out of discriminations and the refusal of human rights, the peace of the world is threatened.

Africa Must Unite, p. 203

Army

IT is not the duty of a soldier to criticise or endeavour to interfere in any way with the political affairs of the country; he must leave that to the politicians, whose business it is. The Government expects you, under all circumstances, to serve it and the people of Ghana loyally.

Address to cadets of the Ghana Military Academy, 18 May 1961

It is not the duty of the army to rule or govern, because it has no political mandate and its duty is not to seek a political mandate. The army only operates under the mandate of the civil government. If the national interest compels the armed forces to intervene, then immediately after the intervention the army must hand over to a new civil government elected by the people and enjoying the people's mandate under a constitution accepted by them. If the army does not do this then the position of the army becomes

dubious and anomalous and involves a betrayal of the people and the national interest.
> Sessional Speech to the National Assembly, Accra. 1 February 1966

Balkanisation

Africa is clearly fragmented into too many small, uneconomic and non-viable States, many of whom are having a very hard struggle to survive.
> *Neo-Colonialism*, p. 25

The political situation in Africa today is heartening and at the same time disturbing. It is heartening to see so many new flags hoisted in place of the old; it is disturbing to see so many countries of varying sizes and at different levels of development, weak and, in some cases, almost helpless. If this terrible state of fragmentation is allowed to continue it may be disastrous for us all.
> *I Speak of Freedom*, p. xiii

So long as we remain balkanised, regionally or territorially, we shall be at the mercy of colonialism and imperialism.
> *Africa Must Unite*, p. 218

The African nations, having learnt their lessons from the past, are no longer prepared to be pawns to foreign nations and to allow their independence and freedom to be sold on the altar of international politics.
> Undated Speech

Balkanisation is the major instrument of neo-colonialism and will be found wherever neo-colonialism is practised.
> *Neo-Colonialism*, p. 14

Black Power

The close links forged between Africans and peoples of African descent over half a century of common struggle continue to inspire and strengthen us. For although the outward forms of our struggle may change, it remains in essence the same, a fight to the death against oppression, racism and exploitation.
> *The Spectre of Black Power*, Introduction

Black Power is part of the world rebellion of the oppressed against the oppressor, of the exploited against the exploiter .... It is linked with the Pan-African struggle for unity on the African continent, and with all those who strive to establish a socialist society.
> The same, p. 10

Black Power gives the African-American an entirely new dimension. It is a vanguard movement of black people, but it opens the way for all oppressed masses.

> The same, p. 12

It must be understood that liberation movements in Africa, the struggles of Black Power in America or in any other part of the world, can only find consummation in the political unification of Africa, the home of the black man and people of African descent throughout the world.

> The same, p. 14

The spectre of Black Power has taken shape and form and its material presence fights to end the exploitation of man by man.

> The same

What is Black Power? By Black Power we mean the power of the four-fifths of the world population which has been systematically damned into a state of undevelopment by colonialism and neo-colonialism. In other words, Black Power is the sum total of the economic, cultural and political power which the black man must have in order to achieve his survival in a highly developed technical society and in a world ravaged by imperialism, colonialism, neo-colonialism and fascism.

> Message to the Black People of Britain, *The Struggle Continues*, p. 7

Black Power epitomises a new stage of revolutionary consciousness of the yearning and aspiration of the black man.

> The same

Real black freedom will only come when Africa is politically united. It is only then that the black man will be free to breathe the air of freedom, which is his to breathe, in any part of the world.

> The same, p. 8

Capitalism

The philosophy of European capitalism in the colonies is that colonial subjects should labour under any foreign government, with uncomplaining satisfaction. They are supposedly "incapable" of developing the resources of their own country, and are taught to labour and appreciate European manufactured goods, so as to become "good" customers.

> *Towards Colonial Freedom*, p. 18

Capitalism is a development by refinement from feudalism, just as feudalism is a development by refinement from slavery.
Consciencism, p. 72

Capitalism is but the gentlemen's method of slavery.
The same

A standard ruse of capitalism today is to imitate some of the proposals of socialism, and turn this imitation to its own use. Running with the hare and hunting with the hounds is much more than a pastime to capitalism; it is the hub of a complete strategy.
The same

Capitalism at home is domestic colonialism.
The same, p. 74

The presuppositions and purposes of capitalism are contrary to those of African society. Capitalism would be a betrayal of the personality and conscience of Africa.
The same

Capitalism is unjust; in our newly independent countries it is not only too complicated to be workable, it is also alien.
The same, p. 76

Capitalism contains many paradoxes, all of them based on the concept of commodity production: the few rich and many poor, poverty and hunger amid superabundance;

"freedom from hunger" campaigns and subsidies for restriction of crop output. But perhaps the most ludicrous is the constant traffic in the same kinds of goods, products and commodities between countries. Everyone is busy, as it were, taking in the other's washing.

Neo-Colonialism, p. 43

Civil Service

The sole test of a civil servant's conduct should be his ability to perform the tasks which are entrusted to him. Anything else is entirely immaterial.

> Speech in the Legislative Assembly on the Motion for Approval of the Government's Revised Constitutional Proposals. 12 November 1956

The fundamental virtues of a civil servant are punctuality, unfailing courtesy, a pleasant disposition, modesty and willingness to serve the public at all times. It must be said of him: he is so efficient and hard-working and yet so humble. These virtues we naturally expect you to uphold in the performance of your duties, whether these be in your offices, workshops, garages, hospital wards, post office and customs' counters, railway booking offices or elsewhere.

> Speech at the Seminar for Senior Civil Servants at Winneba, 14 April 1962

The civil service, being the administrative arm of government, is the instrument for putting into effect the economic and social programme of the government. It is through its machinery that the political platform of the party in power is given effective implementation.

> *Africa Must Unite*, p. 88

I am averse to our civil servants being lodged in the state apparatus like a nail without a head: once you drive it in you cannot pull it out. Government must retain the right of dismissal, and the civil servant must be made to realise that he can be dismissed if he does not perform the job required of him. He must be grappling with his work all the time, thinking twenty-four hours a day how best he can serve his country.

> The same, p. 98

Co-existence

East or West, if we pursue the true interests of the masses of the world this will not only put a stop to war and liquidate colonialism but will end all forms of exploitation and oppression of man by man and of nation by nation, resulting in peaceful co-existence, and the prosperity and happiness of mankind.

> Speech at Conference of Heads of State of Government of Non-Aligned Countries, Belgrade. 1–6 September 1961

There can be no co-existence between African independence and imperialist and neo-colonialist domination; between independent Africa and racist, minority, settler Governments.

> Africa Day Special Message, *The Struggle Continues*, p. 10

Until colonialism and imperialism in all their various forms and manifestations have been completely eradicated from Africa, it would be inconsistent for the African Revolution to co-exist with imperialism.

> The same, p. 204

Just as there can be competing ideologies in the same society, so there can be opposing ideologies between different societies. However, while societies with different social systems can co-exist, their ideologies cannot. There is such a thing as peaceful co-existence between states with different social systems; but as long as oppressive classes exist, there can be no such thing as peaceful co-existence between opposing ideologies.

Consciencism, p. 57

Colonialism

I have always regarded colonialism as the policy by which a foreign power binds territories to herself by political ties with the primary object of promoting her own economic advantage.

Autobiography, Nelson, London, 1957 Preface, p. vii

One of the spurious axioms of colonialism is that those who carry out the policy of the colonial power, however well intentioned they may be, almost always subconsciously seek a solution to the problems of the colonial territory in the terms of a solution which was applicable to the so-called mother country.

Speech in the National Assembly on the eve of Independence. 5 March 1957

The basis of colonial territorial dependence is economic, but the basis of the solution of the problem is political. Hence political independence is an indispensable step towards securing economic emancipation.

Towards Colonial Freedom, Introduction p. xv

We have for too long been the victims of foreign domination. For too long we have had no say in the management of our own affairs or in deciding our own destinies. Now times have changed, and today we are the masters of our own fate.

Speech at Conference of Independent African States Accra. 15 April 1958

The stage opens with the appearance of missionaries and anthropologists, traders and concessionaires, and administrators. While the "missionaries" with "Christianity" perverted implore the colonial subject to lay up "his treasures in Heaven where neither moth nor rust doth corrupt", the traders and concessionaires and administrators acquire his mineral and land resources, destroy his arts, crafts and home industries.

The same, p. 13

The only solution to the colonial problem is the complete eradication of the entire economic system of colonialism, by colonial peoples, through their gaining political independence.

>The same, p. 20

There is abundant proof that the primary motives underlying the quest for colonies and the present administrative and economic policies of the colonial powers are rooted in economic exploitation and not in humanitarianism.

>The same, p. 26

Colonialism and its attitudes die hard, like the attitudes of slavery, whose hangover still dominates behaviour in certain parts of the Western hemisphere.

>*Africa Must Unite*, p. 1

The social effects of colonialism are more insidious than the political and economic. This is because they go deep into the minds of the people and therefore take longer to eradicate. The Europeans relegated us to the position of inferiors in every aspect of our everyday life. Many of our people came to accept the view that we were an inferior people.

>The same, p. 32

We in Africa are living in the most momentous era of our history. In a little less than one
decade the majority of the territories in our
continent have emerged from colonialism
into sovereignty and independence. In a few
years from now we can envisage that all
Africa will be free from colonial rule. Nothing
can stem our onward march to Independence
and freedom.
> Speech at the Cairo Summit Conference, 26 July 1964

We must be vigilant, for colonialism and
imperialism may come to Africa in different
guises. We must therefore alert ourselves to
be able to recognise this whenever and wherever it rears it head and prepare ourselves to
fight against it.
> Undated Speech

In both slavery and feudalism, workers, the
people whose toil transforms nature for the
development of society, are dissociated from
any say in rule. By a vicious division of
labour, one class of citizen toils and another
reaps where it has not sown. In slave and
feudal society the fruit-eaters are not the
fruit-growers. This is the cardinal factor of
exploitation, that the section of society whose
labours transform nature is not the same as

the section which is better fulfilled as a result of the transformation.

Consciencism, p. 71

I distinguish between two colonialisms, between a domestic one and an external one. Capitalism at home is domestic colonialism.

The same, p. 74

I have always believed that the basis of colonialism is economic, but the solution of the colonial problem lies in political action, in a fierce and constant struggle for emancipation as an indispensable first step towards securing economic independence and integrity.

The same, p. 99

It is far easier for the proverbial camel to pass through the needle's eye, hump and all, than for an erstwhile colonial administration to give sound and honest counsel of a political nature to its liberated territory.

The same, p. 102

Once a colony has become nominally independent it is no longer possible, as it was in the last century, to reverse the process. Existing colonies may linger on, but no new colonies will be created.

Neo-Colonialism, Introduction, p. ix

Colonialism has achieved a new guise. It has become neo-colonialism, the last stage of imperialism.

The same, p. 31

Possession of colonies gives a guarantee to the financial oligarchy of the owning country of the monopoly of actual and potential sources of raw materials and outlets for manufactured goods.

The same, p. 83

Commonwealth

We believe that the Commonwealth will gain its greatest strength and influence from an association of nations, each and every one of which is fully sovereign and independent, and totally free from any external direction.

Speech in Accra. 9 January 1950

Freely associated communities make better friends than those associated by subjugation.

Motion of Destiny Speech. 10 July 1953

Today the Commonwealth is no longer an association of like-minded peoples who have derived their political and legal institutions from Britain … . The Commonwealth is now neither a military organisation nor a family looking to Britain to dispense injunctions and approval or disapproval. We must make it clear that the bonds which unite us are those of genuine respect for the absolute political independence of the various independent states constituting the Commonwealth.

> Speech at the Commonwealth Prime Ministers' Conference, London 9 July 1965

Consciencism

With Independence a new harmony needs to be forged, a harmony that will allow the combined presence of traditional Africa, Islamic Africa and Euro-Christian Africa, so that this presence is in tune with the original humanist principles underlying African society … . Such a philosophical statement I propose to name philosophical consciencism, for it will give the theoretical basis for an ideology whose aim shall be to contain the African experience of Islamic and Euro-Christian presence as well as the experience of the traditional African society, and, by gestation, employ them for the harmonious growth and development of that society.

Consciencism, p. 70

Consciencism is the map in intellectual terms of the disposition of forces which will enable African society to digest the Western and the Islamic and the Euro-Christian elements in Africa, and develop them in such a way that they fit into the African personality.

> The same, p. 79

The cardinal ethical principle of philosophical consciencism is to treat each man as an end in himself and not merely as a means. This is fundamental to all socialist or humanist conceptions of man.

> The same, p. 95

Convention People's Party

In all political struggles there come rare moments, hard to distinguish but fatal to let slip, when all must be set upon a hazard, and out of the simple man is ordained strength.

> Speech announcing the formation of the Convention People's Party, Accra. 12 June 1949

Mass movements are well and good but they cannot act with purpose unless they are led and guided by a vanguard political party.

> Autobiography, Preface, p. ix

In our party all are equal regardless of their race or tribe. All are free to express their views. But once a majority decision is taken, we expect such a decision to be loyally executed, even by those who might have opposed that decision. This we consider and proclaim to be the truest form of Democratic Centralism — decisions freely arrived at and loyally executed.

> Speech at Accra Arena to celebrate 10th anniversary of the founding of the CPP, 12 June 1959

Members of the Party must be the first to set an example of all the highest qualities in the nation. We must excel in our field of work by working really hard. We must produce unimpeachable evidence of integrity, honesty, selflessness and faithfulness in the positions in which we are placed by the Party in service to the nation. We must abandon ridiculous ostentation and vanity when the Party has charged us with eminent offices of state, and remember constantly that we hold offices not in our own right, but in the right of the total membership of the Convention People's Party, the masses of the people who really matter.

> The same

The Convention People's Party is in structure democratic and socialistic in philosophy. We have no place in our ranks for the racialist and tribalist. We intend to take drastic steps to expurgate all these and other reactionary tendencies, and we shall not hesitate to expel from our ranks anybody who propagates or spreads in the slightest degree racial and tribal chauvinism. In our Party all are equal regardless of their race or tribe. None is privileged and no one shall escape disciplinary action. For the strength of our Party depends upon its discipline.

The same

These (CPP) aims embrace the creation of a welfare state based upon African socialist principles, adapted to suit Ghanaian conditions, in which all citizens, regardless of class, tribe, colour or creed, shall have equal opportunity, and where there shall be no exploitation of man by man, tribe by tribe, or class by class. Our Party also seeks to promote and safeguard popular democracy based on universal suffrage —"one man, one vote!".

The same

The Convention People's Party is Ghana. Our Party not only provides the Government but is also the custodian which stands guard over the welfare of the people.

> The same

The aim of our Party is to develop our economy, modernise our agriculture and industrialise Ghana. The Party intends to free Ghana from a system of colonial economy and create a system of independent economy. Our ultimate objective is the creation of a socialist society, for we believe that only in such a society will our people have the opportunity of making the maximum contribution to health, happiness and prosperity of our society as a whole.

> The same

I want it to be firmly understood that it is the Convention People's Party which makes the Government and not the government which makes the Convention People's Party, and we intend to give acknowledgement to this fact by raising the prestige of our Party to its proper status in our national structure.

> Speech made in Accra. 12 June 1960

Our mission to Ghana and to Africa and the unique personality of our Party as a vanguard of the African liberation movement impose upon us increasing responsibility, not only to set our own house in order but also to set very high standards, from which all who seek to emulate us shall draw devotion and inspiration in their own struggle.

> Dawn broadcast. 8 April 1961

Members of Parliament must remember at all times that they are representatives of their constituencies only by reason of their Party membership and that on no account should they regard constituency representation as belonging to them in their own right. In other words, constituencies are not the property of Members of Parliament. It is the Party that sends them there and fights for them to become Members of Parliament. I am sure that from now on all Parliamentarians will be guided accordingly in their conduct of representing the Party in Parliament.

> The same

A Party is as strong as the integrity and the sense of discipline and dedication which the membership displays. The example shown in the leadership is reflected in the discipline and dedication demonstrated by the rank and file.

> Message to the seminar for Party officials and members of Parliament, Winneba, 2 December 1962

Our Party has always been the Party of the people, whose welfare has ever been our overriding care. We have always been close to the people, for we have come from them.

> The same

"Seek ye first the political kingdom" became the principal slogan of the CPP, for without political independence none of our plans for social and economic development could be put into effect.

> *Africa Must Unite*, p. 50

In the early years of the CPP and frequently since, I urged members to follow the advice of the Chinese —

"Go to the people
Live among them
Learn from them
Love them
Serve them
Plan with them
Start with what they know
Build on what they have".

> The same, p. 55

The Party gains strength with the masses if it practises inner Party democracy and self-criticism. All members of our Party should be encouraged in every possible way to take an active part in discussing all major questions of Party life. If this is done, it will follow conclusively that all decisions of the Party are decisions of the entire membership who will correctly understand and appreciate them. Democracy will then be at its plenitude throughout all the levels of our Party. I must once again emphasise that the masses of the people form the backbone of our Party and their living conditions and their welfare must be paramount in everything we do. It is for them in particular and Africa in general that our Party exists.

> Speech at the 14th anniversary of the Convention People's Party. 12 June 1963

Our Party must ever be concerned with multiplying and strengthening its contacts with the masses of the people and winning their confidence as their defenders against the evils of poverty, disease, hunger, ignorance and squalor to whose elimination we are dedicated.

> The same

Some of us very easily forget that we ourselves have risen from amongst the masses. We must avoid any conduct that will breed antagonism and uneasy relations. Let us always keep in mind the fact that constant examination and correction are necessary for maintaining the solidarity of the Party. The aim of all correction, however, must be to build and not to destroy.

Broadcast. 11 April 1964

The Convention People's Party is the servant of the people and therefore the men whom it puts into office and power must use that opportunity to serve the people, remembering at all times that selfless and loyal service is a reward in itself.

Speech made in Cape Coast. 1964

A new Party, militant, dynamic and revolutionary had to be formed to mobilise the chiefs and people into a force capable of turning the scales in our favour. It was one of the rare moments in our history — delicate and fearful. The future of our Country, its fate and fortunes, hung desperately in the balance. It was in these circumstances that I decided to form the Convention People's Party.

Address to the National Assembly, 12 June 1965

It was on the 12th of June, 1949, that the masses of our people witnessed the coming into being of the Convention People's Party. It was a time of great political awakening, and our Party was destined to lead the people to victory. This revolutionary Party of ours was to rekindle the torch of African nationalism and blaze the way to the total emancipation and unity of our continent.

<small>The same</small>

Development Plans

Our aim is to make this country a worthy place for all its citizens, a country that will be a shining light throughout the whole continent of Africa, giving inspiration far beyond its frontiers. And this we can do by dedicating ourselves to unselfish service to humanity.

<small>Motion of Destiny Speech. 10 July 1953</small>

What other countries have taken three hundred years or more to achieve, a once dependent territory must try to accomplish in a generation if it is to survive. Unless it is, as it were, "jet propelled", it will lag behind and thus risk everything for which it has fought.

<small>*Autobiography*, Preface, p. x</small>

No man is born a criminal; society makes him so, and the only way to change things is to change the social conditions.
> The same, p. 132

We shall measure our progress by the improvement in the health of our people; by the number of children in school, and by the quality of their education; by the availability of water and electricity in our towns and villages, and by the happiness which our people take in being able to manage their own affairs. The welfare of our people is our chief pride, and it is by this that my Government will ask to be judged.
> Broadcast to the Nation. 24 December 1957

We reject the carping of those critics who judge us merely by the heights which we have achieved and not the depths from which we started.
> Speech at Accra Arena to celebrate the anniversary of the founding of the CPP. 12 June 1959

Steadily and consistently we are building up a better and richer life for our people and our country. We are developing a society free from racial discrimination, a society in which people of different continents and different religious sects and beliefs can work together without molestation, a society in which the relation between man and man is fundamentally based on the social process of production. If we continue to maintain this harmony and work together for the common good, the plans which the Government has already set in motion for our progress, happiness and development will bear rich fruit for us all.

> Broadcast on the eve of Ghana's 16th Independence Anniversary. 6 March 1963

We are in the process of establishing a society in which men and women will have no anxiety about work, food and shelter; where poverty and illiteracy no longer exist and where disease is brought under control; where our educational facilities provide our children with the best possible opportunities for learning; where every person uses his talents to their fullest capacity and contributes to the general well-being of the nation.

> Speech to businessmen at Flagstaff House. 22 February 1963

I will not hide the fact that I am impatient when it comes to building Ghana, and this task rests on the shoulders of my colleagues in the Government. We have to get on with the job resolutely in order to fulfil our promises to the people. Each Minister must regard himself as a managing director and get his particular job done in the allotted time, and properly done. Success follows organisation and inauguration. Real difficulties leading to legitimate delay always receive understanding consideration. But the driving urge to succeed must permeate every branch of government, stemming from the ministerial fountain-head, who must combine a high sense of responsibility with a high sense of urgency. Ministers and Party officials must show themselves as examples to the people by their devotion to their work, by simple living, by leading in service.

> Speech at 14th anniversary of the Convention People's Party, 12 June 1963

The initiative of Ghanaian businessmen will not be cramped, but we must take steps to see that it is channelled towards desirable social ends and is not expended in the exploitation of the community. The Government will encourage Ghanaian businessmen to join with each other in co-operative forms of organisation. In this way Ghanaian businessmen will be able to contribute actively in broadening the vitality of our economy and co-operation, and will provide a stronger form of organisation than can be achieved through individual small businesses.

> Speech at the launching of the Seven-Year Development Plan. 11 March 1964

One can compromise over programme, but not over principle. Any compromise over principle is the same as an abandonment of it.

> *Consciencism*, p. 57

We have the blessing of the wealth of our vast resources, the power of our talents and the potentialities of our people. Let us grasp now the opportunities before us and meet the challenge to our survival.

> Address to the National Assembly. 26 March 1965

Countrymen, the task ahead is great indeed, and heavy is the responsibility; and yet it is a noble and glorious challenge — a challenge which calls for the courage to dream, the courage to believe, the courage to dare, the courage to do, the courage to envision, the courage to fight, the courage to work, the courage to achieve — to achieve the highest excellencies and the fullest greatness of man. Dare we ask for more in life?

    Address to the National Assembly. 12 June 1965

We welcome foreign investment provided that there are no strings attached to it, and also provided that it fits in with our plans for national development and our socialist policy. And we insist that foreign investment should not interfere or meddle with the political life of our country.

    Sessional Address to the National Assembly. 1 February 1966

Economic Independence

Wherever there is economic dependence there is no freedom.

    Towards Colonial Freedom, p. 17

All dependent territories are backward in education, in agriculture and in industry. The economic independence that should follow and maintain political independence demands every effort from the people, a total mobilisation of brain and manpower resources.

    Autobiography, Preface, p. x

Once political independence has been achieved, the country's full potentialities can, and must, be explored. The domestic economy must be planned to promote the interests of its own nationals; and new and wider economic links must be created with other countries. Otherwise the newly independent country may fall victim to the highly dangerous forces of economic imperialism, and find that it has merely substituted one kind of colonialism for another.

Africa Must Unite, p. 108

Something in the nature of an economic revolution is required. Our development has been held back for too long by the colonial-type economy. We need to reorganise entirely, so that each country can specialise in producing the goods and crops for which it is best suited.

Neo-Colonialism, p. 25

Economic Unity

Few would argue against the need for economic planning on a national scale. How much stronger is the argument for continental planning.

Neo-Colonialism, p. 25

In the process of obtaining economic unity there is bound to be much hard bargaining between the various States. Integration of different aspects of economic policy will proceed at different rates, and there may be disappointing delays and compromises to be worked out. But given the will to succeed, difficulties can be resolved.

> The same, p. 28

The foreign firms who exploit our resources, long ago saw the strength to be gained from acting on a Pan-African scale … . The only effective way to challenge this economic empire and to recover possession of our heritage, is for us also to act on a Pan-African basis, through a Union Government.

> The same, p. 259

Education

Above all, don't become know-alls, for nothing is more objectionable and nothing makes one look more of a fool. Education makes us humble and tolerant.

> Address to boys of Adisadel College. 10 November 1955

True academic freedom — the intellectual freedom of the university — is everywhere fully compatible with service to the community: for the university is and must always remain, a living, thinking and serving part of the community to which it belongs.

> Speech made at the University of Ghana, Legon. 24 February 1963

Education consists not only in the sum of what a man knows, or the skill with which he can put this to his own advantage. In my view, a man's education must also be measured in terms of the soundness of his judgment of people and things, and in his power to understand and appreciate the needs of his fellow-men, and to be of service to them. The educated man should be so sensitive to the conditions around him that he makes it his chief endeavour to improve those conditions for the good of all.

> Speech at the opening of the Institute of African Studies. 25 October 1963

We have been doing a great deal to make education available to all. It is equally important that education should seek the welfare of the people and recognise our attempts to solve our economic, cultural, technological and scientific problems.

We look to the Universities to set an example by their efficiency and their sense of responsibility in the use of public funds. They must also set an example in loyalty to the Government and the people, in good citizenship, public morality and behaviour.

The same

Unless science is used for the betterment of mankind, I am at a loss to understand the reason for it all. It does not require a clever brain to destroy life. In fact any fool can do that. But it takes brains — and extraordinarily brilliant brains — to create conditions for human happiness and to make life worth living.

Speech at the Academy of Sciences, Accra. 30 November 1963

Freedom

The peoples of the colonies must have the right to elect their own government, a government without restrictions from a foreign power. We say to the peoples of the colonies that they must strive for these ends by all means at their disposal.

Declaration to the Colonial Peoples of the World. Adopted by Fifth Pan-African Congress, Manchester, England. 15–21 October 1945

The history of colonial liberation movements shows that the first essential thing is ORGANISATION. Some may say unity, but unity presupposes organisation. At least, there must be organisation to unify the country; one person cannot do it; a few leaders cannot do it, but when the masses and the, leaders share common ideals and purposes they can come together in an organisation, regardless of tribal and other differences, to fight for a cause.

Accra Evening News. 18 May 1949

No section of this country should be left unorganised. No individual person should be without membership in some organisation. We must organise as never before, for organisation decides everything.

The same. 14 January 1949

The right of people to decide their own destiny, to make their way in freedom, is not to be measured by the yardstick of colour or degree of social development. It is an inalienable right of peoples which they are powerless to exercise when forces, stronger than they themselves, by whatever means, for whatever reasons, take this right away from them.

Motion of Destiny Speech. 10 July 1953

Without discipline true freedom cannot survive.
> *Autobiography*, Preface, p. x

I have never regarded the struggle for the Independence of the Gold Coast as an isolated objective but always as part of a general world historical pattern. The African in every territory of this vast continent has been awakened and the struggle for freedom will go on. It is our duty as the vanguard force to offer what assistance we can to those now engaged in the battles that we ourselves have fought and won. Our task is not done and our own safety is not assured until the last vestiges of colonialism have been swept from Africa.
> The same, p. 290

According to the motto of the valiant *Accra Evening News*, "We prefer self-government with danger to servitude in tranquillity". Doubtless we shall make mistakes as have all other nations. We are human beings, and hence fallible. But we can try also to learn from the mistakes of others so that we may avoid the deepest pitfalls into which they have fallen. Moreover, the mistakes we may make will be our own mistakes, and it will be our responsibility to put them right. As long as we are ruled by others we shall lay our mistakes at their door and our sense of responsibility will remain dulled. Freedom brings responsibilities, and our experience can be enriched only by the acceptance of these responsibilities.

> Motion of Destiny Speech. 10 July 1953

As long as a single foot of African soil remains under foreign domination, the world shall know no peace.

> Speech in UN General Assembly, New York, 23 September 1960

I do not know how anyone can refuse to acknowledge the right of men to be free.

> *I Speak of Freedom*, p. 5

We in Ghana are waging a relentless war against colonialism, and we shall not rest until every inch of African soil is free and independent. We must drum it again and again into the ears of those who refuse to listen that Africa is not an extension of Europe, and never will be. The colonialists must be warned to keep their hands off Africa. Africa is wide awake and will no longer tolerate or submit to any form of domination whatsoever. Today, in the entire continent of Africa, from Algiers to Cape Town, from Lobito to Lusaka, Africa's Freedom Fighters are up in arms and will lay down their lives rather than their arms in the struggle for total liquidation of colonialism. Protracted constitutional devices designed to defeat the attainment of freedom and independence will no longer be tolerated.

> Speech at the Conference of Heads of State or Government of Non-Aligned Countries, Belgrade, 1–6 September 1961

Freedom without law is anarchy.

> *I Speak of Freedom*, p. 58.

When I talk of freedom and independence for Africa, I mean that the vast African majority should be accepted as forming the basis of government in Africa.

> The same, p. 175

The peoples of the colonies know precisely what they want. They wish to be free and independent, to be able to feel themselves on an equal with all other peoples, and to work out their own destiny without outside interference, and to be unrestricted to attain an advancement that will put them on a par with other technically-advanced nations of the world.

> *Towards Colonial Freedom*, p. 42

Statesmen have broadcast the need to respect fundamental freedoms, the right of men to live free from the shadow of fears which cramp their dignity when they exist in servitude, in poverty, in degradation and contempt. They proclaimed the Atlantic Charter and the Charter of the United Nations, and then said that all these had no reference to the enslaved world outside the limits of imperialism and racial arrogance.

Africa Must Unite, Introduction, p. xi

Freedom is not a commodity which is "given" to the enslaved upon demand. It is a precious reward, the shining trophy of struggle and sacrifice.

The same, p. xv

We have to be constantly on the alert, for we are steadfastly resolved that our freedom shall never be betrayed. And this freedom of ours to build our economies, stands open to danger just as long as a single country on the continent remains fettered by colonial rule and just as long as there exist on African soil puppet governments manipulated from afar. Our freedom stands open to danger just as long as the independent states of Africa remain apart.

The same, p. xvii

It is my deep conviction that all peoples wish to be free, and that the desire for freedom is rooted in the soul of every one of us.

> The same, p. 50

The essential forger of the political revolution is a strong well-organised, broadly based political Party, knit together by a programme that is accepted by all the members, who also submit themselves to the Party's discipline. Its programme should aim for "Freedom first".

> The same

Wherever there is the possibility of conflict arising out of discrimination and the refusal of human rights, the peace of the world is threatened.

> The same, p. 203

The emancipation of the African continent is the emancipation of man. This requires two aims: first, the restitution of the egalitarianism of human society, and second, the logistic mobilisation of all our resources towards the attainment of that restitution.

> Consciencism, p. 78

The fortunes of the African revolution are closely linked with the world-wide struggle against imperialism. It does not matter where the battle erupts, be it in Africa, Asia or Latin America, the master-mind and master-hand at work are the same. The oppressed and exploited people are striving for their freedom against exploitation and suppression. Ghana must not, Ghana cannot be neutral in the struggle of the oppressed against the oppressor.

Address to the National Assembly. 12 June 1965

We are prepared to move ahead side by side with African patriots everywhere until Africa is totally free and united under an All-African Union Government.

Undated Speech

When all is said and done, it is the so-called little man, the bent-backed, exploited, malnourished, blood-covered fighter for independence who decides. And he invariably decides for freedom.

Neo-Colonialism, p. 254

Ghana

In our country we have no place for shirkers, we have places for workers, thinkers and doers .... And so before long this country of

ours will be the land of self-help, efficiency and enterprise. It will begin to reap the reward of courage and suffering. It will be the land of opportunity and of active minds.
> Speech at Accra Arena on 43rd birthday

Love Ghana with a passionate love that can offer the highest sacrifice without demur.
> Undated Speech

The name "Ghana" is deeply rooted in ancient African history, especially in the history of the western portion of Africa known as the Western Sudan. It kindles in the imagination of modern African youth the grandeur and the achievement of a great medieval civilisation which our ancestors developed many centuries before European penetration and subsequent domination of Africa began.
> Speech in Legislative Assembly moving the adoption of the Government's White Paper. 18 May 1956

The greatness of Ghana does not lie only in the physical achievement of our development plans but also in the quality of the life of its people.
> Speech at opening of Flying Training School. 11 September 1959

Ghana has no apologies to render to anybody; nor have we any excuses to make. Let me reiterate that our policies have been directed towards the total liberation of Africa from foreign rule.

> Speech in the National Assembly, Accra. 16 December 1959

The independence of Ghana was the first crack in the seemingly impregnable armour of imperialism in Africa. It created and furnished the bridgehead for organised assaults upon colonialism in Africa.

> *Challenge of the Congo*, Introduction, p. xiv

Ghana is out of the gambling house of colonialism and will never return to it again.

> Broadcast from Conakry to the people of Ghana. 13 March 1966

Imperialism

Imperialism knows no law beyond its own interest and it is natural that despite the pretensions of its agents to justice and fair play, they always seek their interests first.

> *Accra Evening News.* 14 November 1949 (from Speech to Gold Coast People's Representative Assembly to discuss the Coussey Proposals)

Imperialism is a fundamental cause of war. An iniquitous system which has generated intense rivalries and conflicts between nations that erupted into open warfare on a major scale in the scramble to secure "a place in the sun" of colonial supremacy, it has today spawned the neo-colonialism which is as busy as ever in creating clashes among the nations.

Africa Must Unite, p. 202

It is not single states or single continents which are undergoing de-colonisation, but the greater portion of the world. It is not one empire which is expiring, but whole system of imperialism which is at bay. It is not individual communities, but the whole of humanity which is demanding a different and better way of for the world's growing millions.

Speech at the Cairo Summit Conference, 26 July 1964

Imperialism, which is the highest state of capitalism, will continue to flourish as long as conditions permit it. Though its end is certain, it can only come about under pressure of nationalist wakening and an alliance of progressive forces which hasten its end and destroy its conditions of existence. It will end when there are no nations and peoples exploiting others; when there are no vested interests exploiting the earth, its fruits and resources for the benefit of a few against the well-being of the many.

Consciencism, p. 57

When Africa becomes economically free and politically united, the monopolists will come face to face with their own working class in their own countries, and a new struggle will arise within which the liquidation and collapse of imperialism will be completed.

Neo-Colonialism, Conclusion, p. 256

For the imperialist, human values count for nothing and are always subordinated to his quest for profit.

Speech at the Fourth Afro-Asian Solidarity Conference, Winneba. 10 May 1965

The liberation of the whole of our continent, and the restoration of freedom and dignity to those of our brothers who are still under the colonial yoke remain our most important and immediate tasks, but we cannot forget that we are an integral part of humanity involved in all conflicts, perils, strivings and hopes of the human race all over the globe.

We cannot ignore the fact that the same imperialist forces which exploit and subvert our independent states, and which exploit and oppress our people in the remaining colonial enclaves of Africa, are the very same forces which breed armed conflicts, civil strife and economic impoverishment on other continents. It would be folly for us to dream of Africa as a peaceful and thriving continent in a world convulsed by armed conflicts, tormented by hunger and disease and continually menaced by imperialist intrigue and aggression.

> Speech at opening of the Summit Conference of the Organisation for African Unity. 21 October 1965

Throughout the world, the escalation of imperialist aggression is making the issues clear, and exploitation can no longer be disguised. In Africa, a point of explosion against imperialism in its various forms has been reached. But only a massive and organised will to fight can spark it off.

> *Handbook of Revolutionary Warfare*, Preface

Imperialism usually resorts to all types of propaganda in order to highlight and exploit differences of religion, culture, race, outlook, and of political ideology among the oppressed masses, or between regions which share a long history of mutual commercial and cultural exchange. Such methods aim to orientate the leaders of the liberation movements towards a brand of nationalism based on petty-minded and aggressive chauvinism, as well as to steer the liberation movement along a reformist path.

Handbook of Revolutionary Warfare, p. 9

No independent state is immune to imperialist intrigue, pressure and subversion as long as imperialism under any guise is left free to operate on the African continent.

The same, p. 29

The people will have no equitable share in national reconstruction and its benefits unless the victory over imperialism in its colonialist and neo-colonialist stages is complete.

The same

Mounting imperialist aggression in Africa foreshadows a decline in the strength of imperialism since the use of violence to maintain imperialist rule invariably sparks off a stronger explosion of revolutionary activity among oppressed peoples, and experience has shown that such movements can be neither destroyed nor contained.

> The same, p. 38

Imperialism and neo-colonialism must be attacked wherever they are operating throughout the world, and protracted people's wars must be fought until victory is achieved.

> *Dark Days in Ghana*, p. 159

If for a while the imperialists appear to be gaining ground, we must not be discouraged. For time is on our side. The permanency of the masses is the deciding factor, and no power on earth can prevent its ultimate decisive effect on the revolutionary struggle.

> The same

Independence

We prefer self government with danger to servitude in tranquillity.

> Motto of *Accra Evening News*, founded 1948

The right of a people to govern themselves is a fundamental principle, and to compromise on this principle is to betray it.

> Motion of Destiny Speech. 10 July 1953

If there is to be a criterion of a people's preparedness for self government, then I say it is their readiness to assume the responsibility of ruling themselves. For who but a people themselves can say when they are prepared?

> The same

Self government is not an end in itself. It is a means to an end, to the building of the good life to the benefit of all, regardless of tribe, creed, colour or station in life. Our aim is to make this country a worthy place for all its citizens, a country that will be a shining light throughout the whole continent of Africa, giving inspiration far beyond its frontiers. And this we can do by dedicating ourselves to unselfish service to humanity. We must learn from the mistakes of others so that we may, in so far as we can, avoid a repetition of those tragedies which have overtaken other human societies.

> The same

The best way of learning to be an independent sovereign state is to be an independent sovereign state.

> Speech in Legislative Assembly moving the adoption of the Government's White Paper. 18 May 1956

Independence

The achievement of freedom, sovereignty and independence is the product of the matter and spirit of our people. In the last resort we have only been able to become independent because we are economically, socially and politically able to create the conditions which made independence possible and any other status impossible.

> Speech in Legislative Assembly moving an address in reply to Speech from the Throne. March 1957

The Independence of Ghana is meaningless unless it is linked up with the total liberation of the African continent.

> Midnight pronouncement of Independence at Polo Ground, Accra, 5–6 March 1957

It is far better to be free to govern, or misgovern yourself than to be governed by anybody else.

> *Autobiography*, Preface, p. ix

We have only been able to become independent because we are economically, socially and politically able to create the conditions which made independence possible and any other status impossible.

> Speech in National Assembly, 6 March 1957

The welfare of one people cannot be given in trust indefinitely to another people, no matter how benevolent the governing power might be.

> Speech to the National Assembly, Accra. 3 September 1958

It would be a great mistake to imagine that the achievements of political independence by certain areas in Africa will automatically mean the end of the struggle. It is merely the beginning of the end of the struggle.

> The same

Political power is the inescapable prerequisite to economic and social power.

> Speech at Accra Arena to celebrate 10th anniversary of founding of the CPP. 12 June 1959

Independence must be free and unfettered, for freedom of action on the part of a sovereign nation is essential.

> Address to the Steering Committee of the All-Africa People's Conference, Accra. 6 October 1959

It is often alleged that colonial peoples are not "ripe" for independence. The facts of history not only contradict this allegation but repudiate it…. Under the colonial powers' "tutelage" the colonies will never be "ripe" for self-government.

Towards Colonial Freedom, p. 37

What right has any colonial power to expect Africans to become "Europeans" or to have 100 per cent literacy before it considers them "ripe" for self government? Wasn't the African, who is now considered "unprepared" to govern himself, "governing" himself before the advent of Europeans?

The same

To the African, the European settler, whether living in South Africa, Kenya, Angola, or anywhere else in Africa, is an intruder, an alien who has seized African land. No amount of arguing about the so-called benefits of European rule can alter the fundamental right of Africans to order their own affairs.

Africa Must Unite, p. 10

I know of no case where self government has been handed to a colonial and oppressed people on a silver platter. The dynamic has had to come from the people themselves. It is a standing joke in Africa that when the British start arresting, independence is just around the corner.

> The same, p. 18

Every movement for independence in a colonial situation contains two elements, the demand for political freedom and the revolt against poverty and exploitation.

> The same, p. 51

Political independence is only a means to an end. Its value lies in its being used to create new economic, social and cultural conditions which colonialism and imperialism have denied us for so long.

> Speech at the Academy of Sciences, Accra, 30 November 1963

The true welfare of a people does not admit of compromise. If we compromise on the true interest of our people the people must one day judge us, for it is with their effort and their sacrifice, with their forbearance and their denial, that independence is won.

> *Consciencism*, p. 103

Independence is of the people; it is won by the people for the people. That independence is of the people is admitted by every enlightened theory of sovereignty. That it is won by the people is to be seen in the successes of mass movements everywhere. That it is won for the people follows from their ownership of sovereignty. The people have not mastered their independence until it has been given a national and social content and purpose that will generate their well-being and uplift.

>   The same, p. 106

The history of human achievement illustrates that when an awakened intelligentsia emerges from a subject people it becomes the vanguard of the struggle against alien rule.

>   *Africa Must Unite*, p. 43

What meaning can independence have for the people if we throw off political bondage only, and remain in economic and mental subservience?

>   Speech at the Fourth Afro-Asian Solidarity Conference, Winneba. 10 May 1965

No imperial power has ever granted independence to a colony unless the forces were such that no other course was possible. ... The very organisation of the forces of independence within the colony was sufficient to convince the imperial power that resistance to independence would be impossible or that the political and economic consequences of a colonial war outweighed any advantage to be gained by retaining the colony.

Neo-Colonialism, Conclusion, p. 258

Our Independence means much more than merely being free to fly our own flag and to play our own national anthem. It becomes a reality only in a revolutionary framework when we create and sustain a level of economic development capable of ensuring a higher standard of living, proper education, good health and the cultural development of all our citizens.

Undated Speech

The machinations of the colonial power will fail wherever the leaders of the struggle for independence maintain a clear spirit of vigilance, and cultivate genuinely revolutionary qualities. Then, and only then, does a truly independent government emerge, dedicated to national reconstruction in the liberated territory, and determined to assist all those engaged in anti-imperialist struggle.

Handbook of Revolutionary Warfare, p. 11

The example of genuine independence is contagious and will help to fortify extensive zones against imperialist aggression.

> The same

Independence must never be considered in itself but as a stage, the very first stage of the people's revolutionary struggle.

> The same, p. 16

Industrialisation

There is much to be done in the country with regard to industrialisation and development. And we need our own specialists to attend to this. See to it that you are on the job when the time comes!

> Address to boys of Adisadel College. 10 November 1955

Africa must be developed industrially, for her own sake and ultimately for the sake of a healthy world economy. This can only happen if the artificial boundaries that divide her are broken down so as to provide for viable economic units, and ultimately a single African unit.

> Speech of welcome at Conference to discuss Positive Action and Security in Africa, Accra. 7 April 1960

We are running against time in Africa; not only have we to eliminate or eradicate the deficiencies of our past, but we must also, in the shortest possible time, attempt to catch up with modern techniques of our time.

> Speech at the Seminar for Senior Civil Servants at Winneba. 14 April 1962

There are those who argue that the conditions and resources of Africa are not suited to industrialisation. In this way they seek to excuse the economic policy of the colonial powers and support the infiltration of neo-colonialism. The argument falls to the ground when the facts are examined.

> *Africa Must Unite*, p. 23

We have here in Africa everything necessary to become a powerful, modern, industrialised continent. United Nations investigators have recently shown that Africa, far from having inadequate resources, is probably better equipped for industrialisation than almost any other region in the world.

> The same

There is absolutely no doubt that the key to significant industrialisation of this continent of ours lies in a union of African States, planning its development centrally and scientifically through a pattern of economic integration.

> The same, p. 170

We in Ghana are committed to the building of an industrialised socialist society. We cannot afford to sit still and be mere passive onlookers. We must ourselves take part in the pursuit of scientific and technological research as a means of providing the basis for our socialist society.

> Speech at the laying of the foundation stone of the atomic reactor at Kwabenya. 25 November 1964

We recognise that our immediate and paramount task is to mobilise our economic potential to the fullest extent. It is only in this way that we can increase our national production and income in order to assure rising living standards to all our people on a sustained and enduring basis for the good of our society. The revolution of "rising expectation" of our peoples presents us with a formidable challenge. This makes it imperative that "speed" should be the watch-word of our economic growth.

> Speech at the ground-breaking ceremony of the aluminium smelter at Tema. 5 December 1964

Africa has failed to make much headway on the road to purposeful industrial development because her natural resources have not been employed for that end but have been used for the greater development of the Western world.

Neo-Colonialism p. 84

Nationalism

If a national movement is to succeed, every man and woman of goodwill must be allowed to play a part.

Autobiography, p. 109

The great wave of nationalism at present sweeping Africa is a fact which should be recognised; it is a force that no one can hold in check.

Speech made in Accra. 1960

The great millions of Africa, and of Asia, have grown impatient of being hewers of wood and drawers of water, and are rebelling against the false belief that Providence created some to be the menials of others.

Africa Must Unite, Introduction, p. ix

We have witnessed the greatest awakening ever seen on this earth of suppressed and exploited peoples against the powers that have kept them in subjection. This, without a doubt, is the most significant happening of the twentieth century.

    The same, p. x

Wherever there is armed struggle against the forces of reaction, the nationalists are referred to as rebels, terrorists, or frequently "Communist terrorists".

    Neo-Colonialism, p. 247

Nationalism is the ideological channel of the anti-colonialist struggle and represents the demand for national independence of colonised peoples. It is a concept most easily grasped by the population of territories where the low level of development of productive forces (and therefore of capitalist implantation), and the absence of indigenous elements in the spheres of political power, are factors that facilitate the formation of a united militant front, one of the primary conditions for a successful liberation movement.

    Handbook of Revolutionary Warfare, p. 24

The nationalist phase is a necessary step in the liberation struggle, but must never be regarded as the final solution to the problem raised by the economic and political exploitation of our people. For nationalism is narrow in its application.

> The same, p. 25

Neo-colonialism

It acts covertly, manoeuvring men and governments, free of the stigma attached to political rule. It creates client states, independent in name but in point of fact pawns of the very colonial power which is supposed to have given them independence.

> *Africa Must Unite*, p. 174

Neo-colonialism has created a situation in Africa which can only be fought and eradicated by armed revolution and armed struggle.

> Speech at the Second Conference of Non-Aligned States, Cairo. 7 October 1964

Any oblique attempt of a foreign power to thwart, balk, corrupt or otherwise subvert the true independence of a sovereign people is neo-colonialist. It is neo-colonialist because it seeks, notwithstanding the acknowledged sovereignty of a people, to subordinate their interests to those of a foreign power.

Consciencism, p. 102

The cajolement, the wheedlings, the seductions and the Trojan horses of neo-colonialism must be stoutly resisted, for neo-colonialism is a latter-day harpy, a monster which entices its victims with sweet music.

The same, p. 105

Under the searchlight of an ideology, every fact affecting the life of a people can be assessed and judged, and neo-colonialism's detrimental aspirations and sleights of hand will constantly stand exposed.

The same

The essence of neo-colonialism is that the State which is subject to it is, in theory, independent and has all the outward trappings of international sovereignty. In reality its economic system and thus its political policy is directed from outside.

Neo-Colonialism, Introduction, p. ix

A State in the grip of neo-colonialism is not master of its own destiny. It is this factor which makes neo-colonialism such a serious threat to world peace.

> The same, p. x

The result of neo-colonialism is that foreign capital is used for the exploitation rather than for the development of the less developed parts of the world. Investment under neo-colonialism increases rather than decreases the gap between the rich and poor countries of the world.

> The same

Neo-colonialism is the worst form of imperialism. For those who practise it, it means power without responsibility, and for those who suffer from it, it means exploitation without redress.

> The same, p. xi

Neo-colonialism, like colonialism, is an attempt to export the social conflict of capitalist countries. The temporary success of this policy can be seen in the widening gap between the richer and the poorer nations of the world.

> The same, p. xii

Neo-colonialism is based upon the principle of breaking up former large united colonial

Neo-colonialism

territories into a number of small non-viable States which are incapable of independent development and must rely on the former imperial power for defence and even internal security. Their economic and financial systems are linked, as in colonial days, with those of the former colonial ruler.

The same, p. xiii

In fact, neo-colonialism is the victim of its own contradictions. In order to make it attractive to those upon whom it is practised it must be shown as capable of raising their living standards, but the economic object of neo-colonialism is to keep those standards depressed in the interest of the developed countries.

The same, p. xv

Neo-colonialism is a millstone around the necks of the developed countries which practise it. Unless they can rid themselves of it, it will drown them.

The same, p. xvi

Neo-colonialism is by no means exclusively an African question. Long before it was practised on any large scale in Africa it was an established system in other parts of the world. Nowhere has it proved successful, either in raising living standards or in ultimately benefiting the countries which have indulged in it.

<small>The same, p. xvii</small>

The less developed world will not become developed through the goodwill or generosity of the developed Powers. It can only become developed through a struggle against the external forces which have a vested interest in keeping it undeveloped.

<small>The same, p. xix</small>

In Africa, all former colonies which have now become independent, including particularly South Africa, are subject in some degree to neo-colonialist pressures which however much they wish to resist they cannot entirely escape, struggle as they may. The difference in reality is between those States that accept neo-colonialism as a policy and those which resist it.

<small>The same, p. 20</small>

In order to halt foreign interference in the affairs of developing countries it is necessary to study, understand, expose and actively combat neo-colonialism in whatever guise it may appear. For the methods of neo-colonialists are subtle and varied. They operate not only in the economic field, but also in the political, religious, ideological and cultural spheres.

> The same, p. 239

"Special warfare" is a concept of General Maxwell Taylor and a military extension of the creed of John Foster Dulles: let Asians fight Asians. Briefly, the technique is for the foreign power to supply the money, aircraft, military equipment of all kinds, and the strategic and tactical command from a General Staff down to officer "advisers", while the troops of the puppet government bear the brunt of the fighting.

> The same, p. 252

Neo-colonialism is not a sign of imperialism's strength but rather of its last hideous gasp. It testifies to its inability to rule any longer by old methods. Independence is a luxury it can no longer permit its subject peoples, so that even what it claims to have "given" it now seeks to take away.

> The same, p. 253

In the same way as the internal crisis of capitalism within the developed world arose through the uncontrolled action of national capital, so a greater crisis is being provoked today by similar uncontrolled action of international capitalism in the developing parts of the world. Before the problem can be solved it must be at least understood. It cannot be resolved merely by pretending that neo-colonialism does not exist.

> The same, Conclusion, p. 256

The danger to world peace springs not from the action of those who seek to end neo-colonialism but from the inaction f those who allow it to continue.

> The same, p. 259

In spite of all good intentions, in spite of our plans, the naked fact, alas, is that Africa is still an impoverished continent, immobilised by the lack of political cohesion, harassed by imperialism and ransacked by neo-colonialism. That is so because our unity is still incomplete and ineffective in the face of grave threats to our existence. What use is it to us then that our continent is so rich in material human resources? Brothers and colleagues, the fault is in ourselves, not in our stars.

> Speech at opening of the Summit Conference of the Organisation for African Unity, 21 October 1961

It is empire-building without a flag. And this is how it works: they (neo-colonialists) see to it that the political power remains in the hands of indigenous reactionaries. They manoeuvre to control the army, the police and even the Intelligence Services. They see to it that the economic institutions of the country are in the hands of their agents, and that economic production is completely controlled by private foreign capital leaving only the infrastructure in the hands of the indigenous population. They divide the Trade Union and other popular movements. When they have gained full control in this way of a client or puppet state, with a client or puppet administration, then they are in a position to do what they like with that territory, its government and its people. If they cannot get their own way, then they engineer political and military coups, to overthrow the regimes and install new reactionary regimes which will carry out their orders.

Undated Speech

Neo-colonialism has no permanent friends. Its only companions are its own interests.

Speech in Conakry, March 1966

The movement for total liberation from imperialism and neo-colonialism is entering a new phase, the phase of an All-African People's Revolutionary armed struggle.

Challenge of the Congo, Preface, p. xi

A state can be said to be a neo-colonialist or client state if it is independent *de jure* and dependent *de facto*. It is a state where political power lies in the conservative forces of the former colony and where economic power remains under the control of international finance capital.

In other words, the country continues to be economically exploited by interests which are alien to the majority of the ex-colonised population but are intrinsic to the world capitalist sector. Such a state is in the grip of neo-colonialism. It has become a client state.

Handbook of Revolutionary Warfare, p. 8

The prerequisite of a correct and global strategy to defeat neo-colonialism is the ability to discover and expose the way in which a state becomes neo-colonialist. For although a neo-colonialist state enjoys only sham independence it is to all outward appearances independent, and therefore the very roots of neo-colonialism must be traced back to the struggle for independence in a colonial territory.

> The same

By the very nature of its essential objective, which is exploitation, neo-colonialism can only flourish in a client state.

> The same, p. 10

Neo-colonialism constitutes the necessary condition for the establishment of welfare States by the imperialist nations. Just as the welfare state is the internal condition, neo-colonialism is the external condition, for the continued hegemony of international finance capital. It is precisely the increasing dependence of the imperialist system on neo-colonialist exploitation on an international scale which renders its existence so precarious, and its future so uncertain.

> The same, p. 12

Both the basic nature of neo-colonialism and the accumulated experience of liberation movements in Africa, Asia and Latin America indicate clearly that the only way for the broad masses to eradicate neo-colonialism is through a revolutionary movement springing from a direct confrontation with the imperialists, and drawing its strength from the exploited and disinherited masses.

> The same, p. 16

Neo-colonialism has created a situation whereby the masses are exploited beyond the "safe" limits of exploitation. The ensuing massive explosion of pent-up discontent can be nothing but violent. The masses seize back their right to political action and make maximum use of it.

> The same, p. 53

Nuclear Weapons

History will never forgive any nation which, for its own ends, has gambled with the life of mankind.

> Speech in Dublin. 18 May 1960

We do not threaten anyone and we renounce the foul weapons that threaten the very existence of life on this planet. Rather we put our trust in the awakening conscience of mankind which rejects this primitive barbarism, and believe firmly in positive action.

> Speech of welcome at Conference to discuss Positive Action and Security in Africa, Accra. 7 April 1960

The growth of nuclear weapons has made out of date the old-fashioned balance of power which rested upon the ultimate sanction of a major war. Certainty of mutual mass destruction effectively prevents either of the great power blocs from threatening the other with the possibility of a world-wide war, and military conflict has thus become confined to "limited wars". For these neo-colonialism is the breeding ground.

> *Neo-Colonialism*, Introduction, p. xi

One Man — One Vote

To the men I say, assist the women to take an active part in the political life of the country, for remember, no country can be truly democratic in which women do not have equality with men.

> *I Speak of Freedom*, p. 7. (Quotation from *The Spectator Daily*, 23 February 1948)

All that we are asking for is that in Africa the majority should form the basis of Government.

> Press Conference in New Delhi, 29 December 1958

The authority to govern a state should spring from the people, and the people's right to exercise these powers is based on the principle of one man one vote.

> Broadcast on 3rd Anniversary of Independence. March 1960

So long as any group on this continent denies the principle of one man one vote, and uses its power to maintain its privilege, there will be insecurity for the oppressors and constant resentment and revolt on the part of the oppressed.

> Speech of welcome at Conference to discuss Positive Action and Security in Africa, Accra, 7 April 1960

No government can continue to impose its rule in the face of the conscious defiance of the overwhelming masses of its people. There is no force, however impregnable, that a united and determined people cannot overcome.

> The same

What the ruling minorities should be afraid of is not that power will fall into the hands of the majority, but that by their own attempt to maintain a social order which can no longer exist, they will themselves be their own executioners.

> Speech in Dublin. 18 May 1960

The first step towards testing the right of rule in communities of mixed races and creeds is to give every adult, irrespective of race and creed the right to vote. When each citizen thereby enjoys equality of status with all others, barriers of race and colour will disappear and the people will mix freely together and will work for the common good.
> *Africa Must Unite*, p. 11

There is no logic except the right of might that can accept the undemocratic rule of a majority by a minority. The predominant racial group must, and will, provide the government of a country.
> The same

Settlers, provided they accept the principle of one man one vote, and majority rule, may be tolerated, but settler minority governments, never. They are a dangerous anachronism, and must be swept away completely and for ever.
> *Handbook of Revolutionary Warfare*, p. 46

One Party State

We in Africa will evolve forms of government rather different from the traditional Western pattern but no less democratic in their protection of the individual and his inalienable rights.

> Speech to the Indian Council on World Affairs.
> 26 December 1958

If the will of the people is democratically expressed in an overwhelming majority for the governing party, and thereby creates a weakening of the accepted two-party pattern, ... the government is obliged to respect the will of the people so expressed. We have no right to divide our mandate in defiance of the popular will.

Africa Must Unite, p. 71

A people's parliamentary democracy with a one-party system is better able to express and satisfy the common aspirations of a nation as a whole, than a multiple-party parliamentary system, which is in fact only a ruse for perpetuating, and covers up, the inherent struggle between the "haves" and the "have-nots".

Consciencism, p. 101

There is a growing tendency towards the establishment of one-party states, and rightly so. Because of our egalitarian society, this development becomes natural and understandable. The multi-party system which exists in Western countries is in fact a reflection of a social cleavage, and the kind of class system which does not exist in African countries.

> Sessional Address to the National Assembly. 1 February 1966

We have established in Ghana a people's parliamentary socialist democracy where the will of the people, expressed through their majority, is supreme. In fact, here in Ghana, political power resides in the people. It is they, and they alone, who make, enshrine and uphold our constitution — the fundamental law of our land.

> The same

A one-party system of government is an effective and safe instrument only when it operates in a socialist society. In other words, it must be a political expression of the will of the masses working for the ultimate good and welfare of the people as a whole.

> The same

A one-party state can only function for the good of the people within the framework of a socialist state or in a developing state with a socialist programme. The government governs through the people, and not through class cleavages and interests. In other words, the basis of government is the will of the people.

The same

Peace

This is no time for hatred and recrimination. We in Ghana are prepared to forget the past and to make any sacrifice of our national sovereignty towards the attainment of world peace.

Broadcast to the Nation. 24 December 1957

God knows that we in Africa are sick and tired of war and strife, for our continent has been for centuries the scene of tribal conflicts and foreign exploitation. Today we have a vested interest in peace.

The same

A new and vigorous approach to the problem of peace and war is needed. The time has come when the destiny of mankind should cease to hang so dangerously on the aims and ambitions of the Great Powers.

Africa Must Unite, p. 198

World peace is not possible without the complete liquidation of colonialism and the total liberation of peoples everywhere. The indivisibility of peace is staked upon the indivisibility of freedom.

> The same, p. 203

Out of the contradictions and conflicts of vested interests, a new international community must emerge. The process may be slow, but it is inevitable. This new international community can only serve mankind if it is firmly established on freedom, equality and interdependence between nations.

> Speech at the Second Conference of Non-Aligned States, Cairo. 7 October 1964

People's Militia

If armed militia are not organised the masses cannot manifest their power in the struggle against the enemy.

> *Handbook of Revolutionary Warfare*, p. 60

The creation of our continental people's militia is the logical consequence of the unfolding of the African liberation struggle, and it is the essential condition for the emergence of a people's free and united Africa.

The same, p. 63

As the people's revolutionary struggle advances, professional armies as such will gradually disappear, until with the achievement of total African liberation and unity, and the establishment of an All African Union Government they will vanish completely. The defence of Africa will then rest entirely on the continental people's militia.

The same, p. 65

The People

There is no force, however formulated, that a united people cannot overcome.

Speech in Accra. 12 June 1949

It is by the people's effort that colonialism is routed, it is by the sweat of the people's brow that nations are built. The people are the reality of national greatness. It is the people who suffer the depredations and indignities of colonialism, and the people must not be insulted by dangerous flirtations with neo-colonialism.

Consciencism, p. 103

Our aim is to build in Ghana a socialist state which accepts full responsibility for promoting the well-being of the masses. Our national wealth must be built up and used in such a way that economic power shall not be allowed to exploit the worker in town or village, but be used for the supreme welfare and happiness of our people. The people, through the state, should have an effective share in the economy of the country and an effective control over it.
> Speech in the National Assembly. 1964

I do not know of any greater satisfaction than honest and efficient service rendered to the people in the best interest of all the people.
> The same

Do we mobilise and rely on the people in the struggle against imperialism in all its forms, or do we relegate the role of the mass of the people to a secondary place in this struggle? I say that only the mass of the people can ensure victory in our struggle.
> Speech at the Fourth Afro-Asian Solidarity Conference, Winneba. 10 May 1965

The mass of the people can never become the agents or partners of neo-colonialism. The function of neo-colonialism is to exploit, not to share with, the people. In like manner, imperialism, the father of neo-colonialism, does not share; it grabs and exploits the people. It is the people, therefore, and only the people, who can save an African or Asian state from neo-colonialism and imperialism.

> The same

Let us remember always that in the final analysis the masses are the final arbiter. They will always choose freedom and justice, as against oppression and corruption.

> Sessional Address to the National Assembly. 1 February 1966

There is one power which no force of arms can overcome, and that power is the enthusiasm and determination of a whole people.

> Speech in Conakry. March 1966

The true nature of the struggle taking place in Africa and the world between the forces of progress and those of reaction (is) in the final analysis ... the fight of the common man against injustice and privilege.

> *Challenge of the Congo*, Preface, p. x

The people are the makers of history and it is they who, in the final analysis, win or lose wars.

Handbook of Revolutionary Warfare, p. 75

The higher the level of a people's political awareness, the greater is their understanding of their historical mission. Africa is ripe for armed revolution.

Dark Days in Ghana, p. 158

In a revolutionary situation it is a crime against the people to forgive those who have betrayed them.

Dark Days in Ghana

Philosophy

Philosophy, in understanding human society, calls for an analysis of facts and events, and an attempt to see how they fit into human life, and so how they make up human experience. In this way, philosophy, like history, can come to enrich, indeed to define, the experience of man.

Consciencism, Introduction, p. i

The critical study of the philosophies of the past should lead to the study of modern theories, for these latter, born of the fire of contemporary struggles, are militant and alive.

The same, p. 5

Practice without thought is blind; thought without practice is empty.

The same, p. 78

Positive Action

When a colonialist country sees the advance of Positive Action, it unfailingly develops a policy of containment, a policy whereby it seeks to check this advance and limit it. This policy often takes the form of conferences and protracted constitutional reforms.

The same, p. 101

The people are the backbone of Positive Action. It is by the people's effort that colonialism is routed, it is by the sweat of the people's brow that nations are built. The people are the reality of national greatness.

The same, p. 103

Without Positive Action, a colonial territory cannot be truly liberated. It is doomed to creep in its petty pace from day to day towards the attainment of a sham independence that turns to dust, independence which is shot through and through with the supreme interest of an alien power.

The same, p. 104

When independence has been gained, Positive Action requires a new orientation away from the sheer destruction of colonialism and towards national reconstruction.

The same, p. 105

If world war is not to occur it must be prevented by Positive Action. This Positive Action is within the power of the peoples of those areas of the world which now suffer under neo-colonialism but it is only within their power if they act at once, with resolution and in unity.

Neo-Colonialism, Conclusion, p. 259

Progress does not come by itself, neither desire nor time can alone ensure progress. Progress is not a gift, but a victory. To make progress, man has to work, strive and toil, tame the elements, combat environment, recast institutions, subdue circumstances, and at all times be ideologically alert and awake.

Address to the National Assembly. 12 June 1965

Propaganda

Propaganda is a means of liberation, an instrument of clarification, information, education and mobilisation.

Handbook of Revolutionary Warfare, p. 95

Our propagandists must leave no problem untackled, no mistake unexposed. Truth must always be told. It is a proof of strength, and even the hardest truth has a positive aspect which can be used.

The same, p. 100

Racialism

The foulest intellectual rubbish ever invented by man is that of racial superiority and inferiority.

Speech made in Accra. 21 June 1952

There is no solution to the race question until all forms of racial discrimination and

segregation anywhere are made criminal offences. Under real socialism, racialism vanishes.
> Message to the Black People of Britain, *The Struggle Continues*, p. 14

We repudiate and condemn all forms of racialism, for racialism not only injures those against whom it is used, but warps and perverts the very people who preach and project it.
> Speech of welcome at Accra Conference of Independent African States. 15 April 1958

Religion

Religion is an instrument of bourgeois social reaction. It is essential to emphasise in the historical condition of Africa that the state must be secular.
> *Consciencism*, p. 13

People who are most aggressively religious are the poorer people; for, in accordance with the Marxist analysis, religion is social, and contemporary religious forms and practices have their main root in the social depression of workers.
> The same

Fear created the gods, and fear preserves them: fear in bygone ages of war, pestilences, earthquakes, and nature gone berserk, fear of "acts of God"; fear today for the equally blind forces of backwardness and rapacious capital.

    The same, p. 14

Revolution

Revolutions are brought about by men ... who think as men of action and act as men of thought.

    Consciencism, p. 23

A revolutionary ideology is not merely negative. It is not a mere conceptual refutation of a dying social order, but a positive creative theory, the guiding light of the emerging social order.

    The same, p. 34

History furnishes innumerable proofs of one of its own major laws, that the budding future is always stronger than the withering past. This has been amply demonstrated during every major revolution throughout history.

    Neo-Colonialism, p. 252

Between a zone under enemy control where the masses are awakening and a highly contested zone, there is only one missing link: a handful of genuine revolutionaries prepared to organise.
> *Handbook of Revolutionary Warfare*, p. 49

There is no fundamental difference between armed struggle as such and organised revolutionary action of a civil type. The various methods of our struggle, and the changing from one method to another should be determined mainly by the circumstances and the set of conditions prevailing in a given territory.
> The same

At this momentous period of history, as the era of people's armed revolution gets under way in Africa, I see coming the triumph of the human spirit, the collapse of the forces of inhumanity and the emergence of the glorious effort finally to free mankind from senseless and inhuman exploitation, degradation and wars.
> *The Spectre of Black Power*, p. 12

Non-violent methods are now anachronistic in revolution.
> The same, p. 13

Revolutionary War

Taking up arms for African freedom and unity is not the product of a cruel, uncouth purpose, it is an art, the crystallisation of serious study and knowledge of the oppressor and the oppressed.

Handbook of Revolutionary Warfare, prelims.

Revolutionary warfare is the logical, inevitable answer to the political, economic and social situation in Africa today. Either we fight together now, or we will each fall in turn unaided and alone to the collective blows of imperialism.

The same, p. 42

The collective and continental nature of our will and our space, the urgency of conquering the initiative and the protracted nature of a guerrilla war calls for a united All-African organisation of all freedom fighters on the African continent.

The same

Our armed struggle for freedom is neither moral nor immoral, it is a scientific historically-determined necessity.

The same, p. 19

The problem is not whether one is born or is not born a natural guerrilla fighter. The problem is not whether guerrillas are naturally suited to Africa, or Africa to guerrilla warfare. Predestination of this sort never exists. The fact is that guerrilla warfare is the only way in which the total liberation and unity of the African continent can be achieved.

> The same, p. 20

We possess the vital ingredient necessary to win; the full and enthusiastic support of the broad masses of the African people who are determined once and for all to end all forms of foreign exploitation, to manage their own affairs, and to determine their own future. Against such overwhelming strength organised on a Pan-African basis, no amount of enemy forces can hope to succeed.

> The same, p. 23

Either we concentrate our forces for a decisive armed struggle to achieve our objectives, or we will each fall one by one to the blows of imperialism in its present stage of open and desperate offensive.

> The same, p. 41

The dimension of our struggle is equal to the size of the African continent itself. It is in no way confined within any of the absurd limits of the micro-states created by the colonial powers, and jealously guarded by imperialist puppets during the neo-colonialist period.

> The same, p. 43

The people's armed struggle, the highest form of political action, is a revolutionary catalyst in the neo-colonialist situation.

> The same, p. 52

Our war is not a war of conquest, it is a war of revolutionary liberation. We fight not only in self-defence but to free, unite and reconstruct.

> The same, p. 67

Military strategy presupposes political aims. All military problems are political, and all political problems are economic.

> The same, p. 15

A revolutionary fails only if he surrenders.

> Letter to an African-American, 1968

The guerrilla is the masses in arms.

> *Handbook of Revolutionary Warfare*, prelims.

Time is on the side of the masses, and nothing can permanently frustrate their ultimate fulfilment.
>   *The Big Lie*, Author's Note

Socialism

We aim at creating in Ghana a socialist society in which each will give, according to his ability, and receive according to his needs.
>   Speech at Accra Arena to celebrate 10th anniversary of the founding of the CPP. 12 June 1959

I have stated on many occasions that the Government's policy is aimed at evolving a socialist pattern of society, no secret has been made of this fact. I have also stated that there are different paths to socialism, that each country must find its own way and that socialism could differ in form from one country to another. Ghana intends to evolve its own socialist pattern of society adapted to its own particular needs.
>   Broadcast. 9 October 1960

Africa's new man must be a man indeed. All this needs a great deal of zeal. Let us remember, however, that our zeal should make us adroit and alert to all the implications of our actions. For we have a tremendous herculean task before us. It needs all our care, all our brains. Our Party, through all its members, must show its merits in this our greatest mision yet — the building of a socialist Ghana.

> Speech made in Accra. 8 April 1964

If one seeks the social-political ancestor of socialism, one must go to communalism. Socialism stands to communalism as capitalism stands to slavery. In socialism, the principles underlying communalism are given expression in modern circumstances.

> *Consciencism*, p. 78

Socialism is a form of social organisation which, guided by the principles underlying communalism, adopts procedures and measures made necessary by demographic and technological developments.

> The same

The passage from the ancestral line of slavery via feudalism and capitalism to socialism can only lie through revolution; it cannot lie through reform. For in reform, fundamental principles are held constant and the details of their expression modified. In the words of Marx, it leaves the pillars of the building intact.

> The same, p. 74

Under socialism ... the study and mastery of nature has a humanist impulse, and is directed not towards a profiteering accomplishment, but the affording of ever-increasing satisfaction for the material and spiritual needs of the greatest number.
> The same, p. 76

The restitution of Africa's humanist and egalitarian principles of society requires socialism. It is materialism that ensures the only effective transformation of nature, and socialism that derives the highest development from this transformation.
> The same, p. 77

When socialism is true to its purpose, it seeks a connection with the egalitarian and humanist past of the people before their social evolution was ravaged by colonialism.
> The same, p. 106

National liberation and the obvious advantages of socialist development for nations evolving out of a colonialist domination and without the capital means for making that development, are major factors determining imperialist strategy towards these nations, in both the interests of its internal struggle and in the fight against socialism.

> *Neo-Colonialism*, p. 55

Socialism is not spontaneous. It does not arise of itself. It has abiding principles according to which the major means of production and distribution ought to be socialised if exploitation of the many by the few is to be prevented; if, that is to say, egalitarianism in the economy is to be protected.

> "African Socialism Revisited", *African Forum*, Vol. 1, No. 3, 1966

Socialism in Africa introduces a new social synthesis in which modern technology is reconciled with human values, in which the advanced technical society is realised without the staggering social malefactions and deep schisms of capitalist industrial society.

> The same

It is the elimination of fancifulness from socialist action that makes socialism scientific. To suppose that there are tribal, national, or racial socialisms is to abandon objectivity in favour of chauvinism.

> The same

We live in a world in which one quarter of the people are becoming richer and richer, while the rest grow poorer and poorer.

This situation can only be remedied by world socialism. For as long as capitalism and imperialism go unchecked there will always be exploitation, an ever-widening gap between the haves and have-nots, and all the evils of imperialism and neo-colonialism which breed and sustain wars.

Challenge of the Congo, Preface, p. x

Socialism and African unity are organically complementary.

Handbook of Revolutionary Warfare, p. 28

Socialism implies:

1. Common ownership of the means of production, distribution and exchange. Production is for use, and not for profit.
2. Planned methods of production by the state, based on modern industry and agriculture.
3. Political power in the hands of the people, with the entire body of workers possessing the necessary governmental machinery through which to express their needs and

aspirations. It is a concept in keeping with the humanist and egalitarian spirit which characterised traditional African society, though it must be applied in a modern context. All are workers; and no person exploits another.
4. Application of scientific methods in all spheres of thought and production.

The same

Socialism must provide a new social synthesis in which the advanced technical society is achieved without the appalling evils and deep cleavages of capitalist industrial society.

The same

There is only one true socialism and that is scientific socialism, the principles of which are abiding and universal. The only way to achieve it is to devise policies aimed at general socialist goals, which take their form from the concrete, specific circumstances and conditions of a particular country at a definite historical period.

The same, p. 29

Only under socialism can we reliably calculate the capital we need for our development, ensure that the gains of investment are applied to the general welfare, and achieve our goal of a free and united continent.

> The same, p. 29

Politics is class struggle.

> *Dark Days in Ghana*

Politics is nothing more than the manifestation of socialist needs in a given class society.

> The same

"Third World"

If we are to achieve revolutionary socialism then we must avoid any suggestion that will imply that there is any separation between the socialist world and a "Third World".

> The Myth of the "Third World", *Two Myths*, p. 76

The oppressed and exploited peoples are the struggling revolutionary masses committed to the socialist world ... . They do not constitute a "Third World". They are part of the revolutionary upsurge which is everywhere challenging the capitalist, imperialist and neo-colonialist power structure of reaction and counter-revolution. There are thus two worlds only, the revolutionary and the counter-revolutionary — the socialist world trending towards communism, and the capitalist world with its extensions of imperialism, colonialism and neo-colonialism.

The same

I do not deny the existence of the struggling "wretched of the earth", but maintain that they do not exist in isolation as a "Third World". They are an integral part of the revolutionary world, and are committed to the hilt in the struggle against capitalism to end the exploitation of man by man.

The same, p. 77

Trade Unionism

We intend to demonstrate that the exploitation of man by man must cease. We also intend to demonstrate that a man is entitled to the fruits of his labour. The Trade Union movement as I see it in Africa is one of the important spearheads for economic and social progress.

Speech at the inauguration ceremony of the All African Regional Conference of the International Confederation of Free Trade Unions, Accra. 14 January 1957

We intend to encourage in Africa not only the dignity of labour in workers' movements, but the dignity of man whose needs constitute the ultimate end of all productive enterprise.

> The same

The Trade Union movement in Africa is indissolubly linked up with the struggle for the political freedom, independence and unity of our continent.

> Speech of welcome to representatives of African Trade Unions meeting in Accra to organise an All-African Trade Union Federation. 5 November 1959

Political freedom and the rights of workers are indivisible.

> The same

Unitary Government

All provincial and tribal differences should be broken down completely. By operating on tribal differences and colonialism, the colonial powers' age-long policy of "divide and rule" has been enhanced, while the colonial national independence movement has been obstructed and bamboozled.

> *Towards Colonial Freedom*, Introduction, p. xv

In order to repair effectively and quickly the serious damage done to Africa as a result of imperialism and colonialism, emergent African states need strong unitary governments capable of exercising a central authority for the mobilisation of the national effort and the co-ordination of reconstruction and progress.

> Telegram to Cyrille Adoula, Congolese Prime Minister. 17 August 1962

United Nations Organisation

It may be argued that the existence of the United Nations Organisation offers a guarantee for the independence and the territorial integrity of all states, whether big or small. In actual fact, however, the UN is just as reliable an instrument for world order and peace as the Great Powers are prepared to allow it to be.

> *I Speak of Freedom*, Preface, p. xii

Ghana regards the faithful adherence to the principles of the United Nations Charter as an integral part of her foreign policy and we shall continue to co-operate in the activities of the United Nations and its specialised agencies.

> Speech in the National Assembly, Accra. 3 September 1958

Women

The women of Africa have already shown themselves to be of paramount importance in the revolutionary struggle. They gave active support to the independence movement in their various countries, and in some cases their courageous participation in demonstrations and other forms of political action had a decisive effect on the outcome. They have, therefore, a good revolutionary record, and are the source of power for our politico-military organisation. Maximum use must be made of their special skills and potentialities.

Handbook of Revolutionary Warfare, p. 89

The degree of a country's revolutionary awareness may be measured by the political maturity of its women.

The same, p. 91

www.ingramcontent.com/pod-product-compliance
Lightning Source LLC
Chambersburg PA
CBHW031713230426
43668CB00006B/195